MARSHALL CAVENDISH
More Science Projects

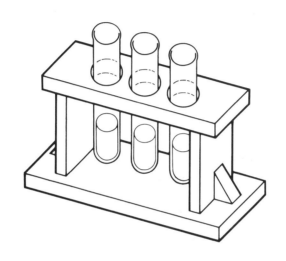

MORE SCIENCE PROJECTS

Astronomy

Written by Peter Lafferty

MARSHALL CAVENDISH
New York · London · Toronto · Sydney

Library Edition Published 1989

Published by Marshall Cavendish Corporation
147 West Merrick Road
Freeport, Long Island
N.Y. 11520

Printed in Italy by L.E.G.O. S.p.A., Vicenza

Library of Congress Cataloging-in-Publication Data

Lafferty, Peter.
   Marshall Cavendish More Science Projects Astronomy / written by
Peter Lafferty : illustrated by Tony Gibbons, Terry Burton.
      p. cm. – (Marshall Cavendish More Science Projects II : 5)
   Summary: Provides an overview of the world of astronomy.
   ISBN 1-85435-180-X. ISBN 1-85435-175-3 (set)
   Astronomy – Juvenile literature. [1. Astronomy.] I. Gibbons, Tony,
ill. II. Burton, Terry, ill. III. Title. IV. Series.
QB46.L34 1989
520–dc20
                                                        89-7184
                                                           CIP
                                                            AC

PICTURE CREDITS
Key: t – Top, b – Bottom

Front Cover: NASA / Science Photo Library

Page 4-5: Dr Fred Espenak / Science Photo Library
Page 8: Robin Scagell / Science Photo Library
Page 9: Jerry Schad / Science Photo Library
Page 12-13: NASA / Science Photo Library
Page 15: The Mansell Collection
Page 16: NASA / Science Photo Library
Page 17 t & 17 b: NASA / Science Photo Library
Page 19: NASA / Science Photo Library
Page 21 t: The Mansell Collection
Page 21 b: NASA / Science Photo Library

Page 24-25: Allan Morton / Dennis Milton / Science
           Photo Library
Page 27: R Royer / Science Photo Library
Page 28: Fred Espenak / Science Photo Library
Page 30: Lick Observatory OP / Science Photo Library
Page 32 & 33: John Stanford / Science Photo Library
Page 34-35: Doug Johnson / Science Photo Library
Page 38: NASA / Science Photo Library
Page 40: George Phillip Ltd
Page 41: Robin Scagell
Page 43: U.S. Naval Observatory / Science Photo
        Library

Artwork by: Tony Gibbons / Bernard Thornton Artists

CONTENTS

STAR-GAZING

If you look at the sky at night, you will see a beautiful sight. Thousands of stars shine overhead. Some are very bright, and some are faint. Most stars look white, but some are faintly colored red, blue, or yellow. Some seem to be grouped together, making a pattern in the sky. The earlier star-gazers thought that one of these groups looked like the shape of a bear, so they called it the Great Bear. They gave names to other groups of stars, too, and to individual stars.

Astronomy is the scientific study of the stars and other objects seen in the sky. People who study the stars are called astronomers. They work in *observatories* and use *telescopes* and other instruments to help them in their work. A telescope is not necessary when you first begin to look at the stars. You can see a lot just with your eyes, if you know what to look for.

You could start by looking at the *planets*. These are worlds that, like the earth, travel around the sun. At night, they look like bright stars, but they do not move across the sky in the same way as stars. As you star-gaze, you might see a "*shooting star*," or *meteor*. It is not a star at all, but a fragment of rock burning up as it enters the earth's atmosphere. You may also see a faint glow of light from a giant group of stars called a *galaxy*, or from a glowing cloud of gas called a *nebula*.

Once you know what to look for and how to make observations, you will be an amateur astronomer. The findings

of amateur astronomers have often helped scientists. Some amateurs have discovered their own *comets*, which have been named for them.

From careful observation of the sky, astronomers have learned a lot about what goes on inside a star, why it shines in the way it does, and what happens when a star is "born" or when it "dies." But many mysteries of the *universe* remain to be solved, especially in the farthest reaches of space.

STAR PATTERNS

The patterns of stars we see in the night sky are called *constellations*. Most of them have names given to them hundreds of years ago by people who imagined they could see the shapes of animals, kings and queens, gods and goddesses. Early astronomers made up stories to explain how the different figures of animals and people came to be placed in the sky, which is why many constellations have names like the Great Bear and Orion.

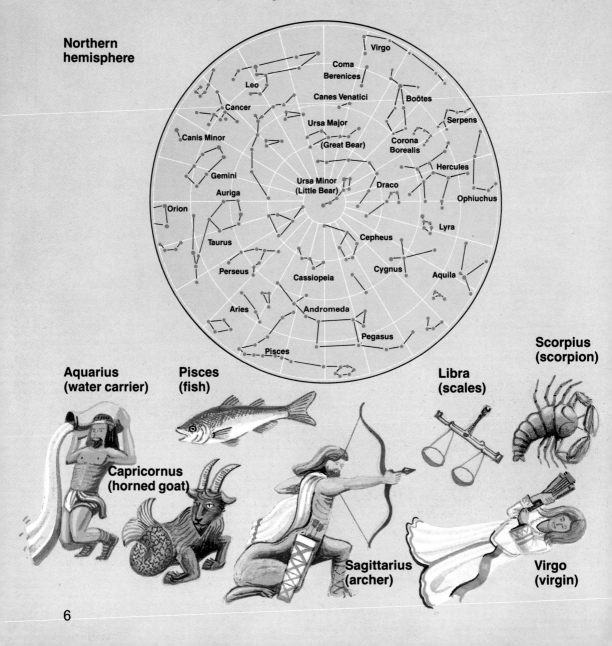

Northern hemisphere

Virgo
Coma Berenices
Leo
Canes Venatici
Boötes
Cancer
Serpens
Ursa Major (Great Bear)
Canis Minor
Corona Borealis
Hercules
Gemini
Ursa Minor (Little Bear)
Draco
Auriga
Ophiuchus
Orion
Lyra
Taurus
Cepheus
Perseus
Cygnus
Aquila
Cassiopeia
Aries
Andromeda
Pegasus
Pisces

Aquarius (water carrier)

Pisces (fish)

Capricornus (horned goat)

Sagittarius (archer)

Libra (scales)

Scorpius (scorpion)

Virgo (virgin)

Signposts

In addition to being an almost complete "book" of the ancient stories, the constellations are useful as "signposts" to help us find our way around the sky. Different signposts are used, depending on where you live on earth. The Great Bear, or Ursa Major, is used in the northern hemisphere, but it cannot be seen from the southern hemisphere. There, constellations such as the Southern Cross are used.

Although the stars in each constellation appear as if they are together, they are sometimes at very different distances away from us. The "end" star of the Great Bear is more than twice as far away from earth as the star next to it in the pattern.

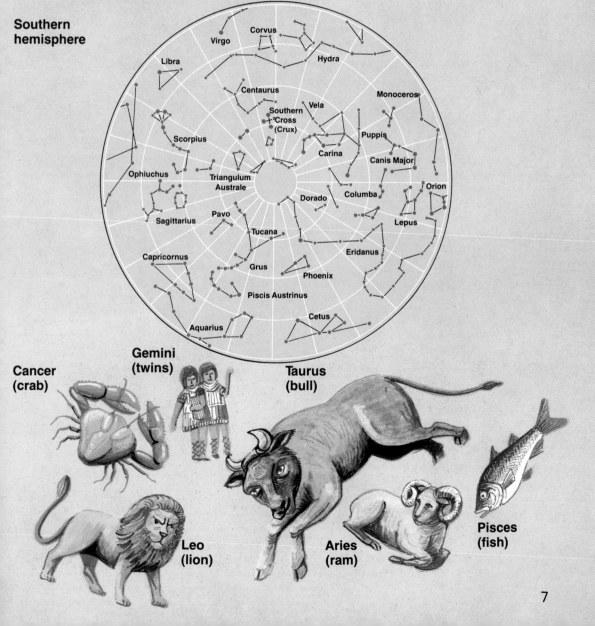

Southern hemisphere

Virgo — Corvus — Hydra — Libra — Centaurus — Vela — Monoceros — Scorpius — Southern Cross (Crux) — Puppis — Carina — Canis Major — Ophiuchus — Triangulum Australe — Dorado — Columba — Orion — Sagittarius — Pavo — Lepus — Tucana — Eridanus — Capricornus — Grus — Phoenix — Piscis Austrinus — Cetus — Aquarius

Cancer (crab)

Gemini (twins)

Taurus (bull)

Leo (lion)

Aries (ram)

Pisces (fish)

7

A good way to begin your observations is to learn how to find certain key constellations. You need no special equipment at first except for a notebook in which to record the stars and constellations that you see, and a compass. Make a sketch of each one showing the position of the stars, and note the date and time.

PROJECT

1

The Big Dipper or Plow

The Big Dipper in Ursa Major is the most useful signpost to star-gazers in Europe and North America, as it can be seen throughout the year. From it, you can find your way to other constellations such as Cassiopeia and Boötes.

STEP **2**

Look at the second star in the handle of the Dipper. This star is called Mizar. It is really two stars close together. Can you see the second faint star? You need a clear, dark night to see it clearly. Imagine a line drawn from Mizar through the North Star. Extend the line until you come to a W- or M-shaped group of five bright stars. This is Cassiopeia.

STEP **3**

Follow the line of the handle of the Dipper about as far again as its length. You will come to a brilliant, faintly orange star called Arcturus. This is in the kite-shaped constellation of Boötes, the Herdsman. The Herdsman is not always visible, as sometimes it is below the horizon.

Cassiopeia

North Star

STEP **1**

When it is dark, go outside and face north. Wait a few minutes until your eyes get accustomed to the dark. You will soon be able to make out the seven stars that make up the Big Dipper, three for the handle and four for the cup. The two equally-bright stars at the end are called the Pointers. An imaginary line drawn through them and carried on to the north leads to another bright star called Polaris, or the North Star. The North Star is almost due north in the sky.

Boötes

Mizar

The Big Dipper

Arcturus

Orion

Orion can only be seen in winter and early spring, but it is the most magnificent constellation in the entire sky at this time of the year. It can be used to find other constellations, such as Canis Major and Taurus.

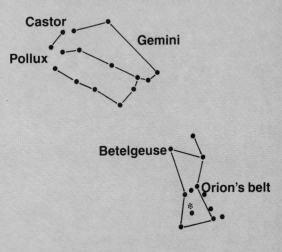

STEP 1

When it is dark, at about 10 pm in January or 8 pm in February, go outside and look toward the south. There, you will see the seven bright stars that make up Orion, the Hunter. The bright, faintly orange-red star near the top left is Betelgeuse. At the bottom right corner is the white star Rigel. The three stars in a line in the middle make up the Hunter's belt.

STEP 2

Imagine a line drawn through Orion's belt and follow it upward. It leads to an orange star, called Aldebaran, in the constellation of Taurus, the Bull. If you follow this imaginary line in the opposite direction, the belt points to Sirius, the brightest star in the sky. Sirius is in the constellation of the Great Dog, Canis Major, and is sometimes called the Dog Star.

STEP 3

Find Betelgeuse at the top of Orion and look upward toward the top left. You should be able to see the constellation of Gemini with the distinct bright pair of stars Castor and Pollux.

Theodolites or astrolabes are used to measure the angle of a star, or any other object, and the latitude and bearing of a star from the north-south meridian. Astrolabes were used by the ancient Arabs to tell the time at night, and sailors used them to navigate by.

Attach two or three washers to a piece of string to make a plumbline. Tie the free end of the string around the head of the nail so the plumbline hangs straight down.

PROJECT

3

Making a theodolite

You will need a drinking straw, a protractor, a compass, glue, string, washers, a wooden post 4 inches (10 cm) long and 1 inch (2 cm) square, thick cardboard, a piece of hardboard, nails and screws.

STEP 1

Attach the drinking straw to the base of a protractor with glue. Make a hole in the center of the bottom of the protractor and hammer a nail through the protractor into the post. Leave the head of the nail sticking out in the front of the protractor so that the protractor can move easily.

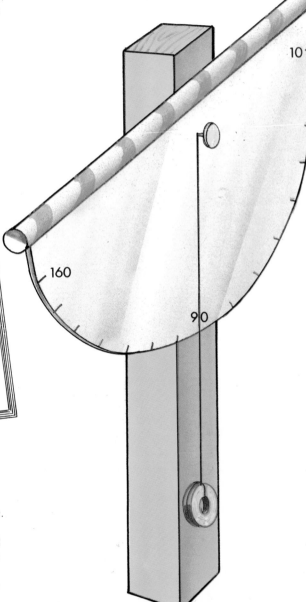

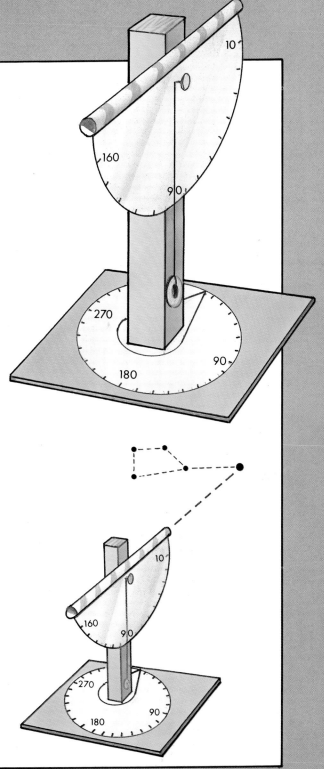

STEP 2

Cut a large circle out of thick cardboard and mark the angles of a circle from 0° to 360°. Cut out a cardboard pointer and color it. Glue the circle on the piece of hardboard and make a hole in the center. Make a hole in the wide end of the pointer and place it on top of the cardboard circle with a washer on each side. Screw the hardboard to the bottom of the post as a base plate. Make sure that the base and pointer can move easily. Align the pointer and the 0° sign on the scale with the North Star.

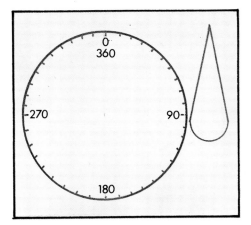

STEP 3

Go outside when it is dark and look toward the North Star. Line up the straw with the North Star. Read the angle on the protractor where the plumbline crosses it, this will give you the altitude of the star. The azimuth, or latitude bearing, is read from the pointer on the base plate. Now choose another star, or constellation, and move the wooden post and straw until the straw lines up with the object. Read the angles for the altitude and azimuth as before. Using these measurements, you can plot the position of stars in the sky.

POWERHOUSE SUN

To us the sun is a special star because we live on one of its family of planets. The sun gives off large amounts of energy in the form of heat and light, and we depend on them to live. It is the powerhouse that supplies all the earth's energy.

The sun is extremely hot. On its surface, the temperature reaches about 10,800°F (6,000°C). Sometimes there are surface areas where the temperature is slightly lower, which show up as dark *sunspots*. But even here the temperature reaches 7,200°F (4,000°C). In the center, the sun's temperature is much higher – around 27,000,000°F (15,000,000°C).

Such high temperatures make the sun a turbulent place. On the surface, or photosphere, eruptions of light, called flares, occur. Immense trails of glowing gas, called *prominences*, are thrown hundreds of thousands of miles into space from the outer layer.

How is this heat and energy made? The sun does not burn in the same way as a coal fire, or it would have run out of "fuel" a long time ago. The answer is that *nuclear reactions* are taking place deep within the sun. In these nuclear reactions, four atoms of a gas called hydrogen are fused together to form one atom of another gas, helium. This produces great amounts of energy.

The sun is made up entirely of gases. Its center consists mainly of hydrogen. Although about 600 million tons of hydrogen are being converted into helium every second, the sun contains such vast amounts of gases that it will continue to burn for thousands of millions of years.

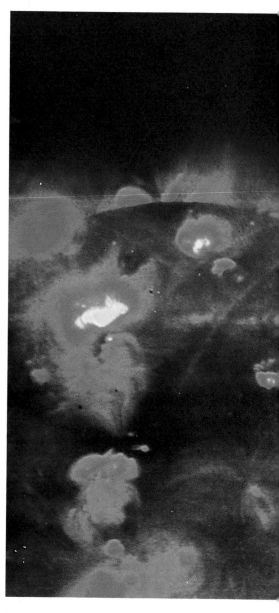

A huge trail of glowing gas, called a prominence, bursts from the sun's surface. The plume of gas is 312,500 miles (500,000 kilometers) long. The earth would fit into its length 40 times.

The earth could easily fit into the sun a million times. But the sun is only an average-sized star, called a dwarf star. About 24 million suns could fit inside a *supergiant* star, the largest and most luminous type found so far. Temperatures inside some of these stars reach 5,400,000,000°F (3,000,000,000°C).

THE SUN'S FAMILY

Ancient astronomers called the planets "wanderers" because they seemed to move around the sky in a strange way. We know now that these wanderings happen because the planets, including the earth, circle around the sun. The planets are part of the sun's "family", which is called the *solar system*. This family also includes smaller objects called *asteroids*, comets, and meteors, which also move around the sun.

Major planets

There are nine planets moving in circular paths called *orbits* around the sun. Closest to the sun is the planet Mercury. It is 36,250,000 miles (58 million km) from the sun. Then come Venus, earth, Mars, Jupiter, Saturn, Uranus, Neptune, and Pluto, which is 3,700 million miles (5,900 million km) from the sun. Some of the planets, like earth, have moons circling around them.

Minor planets, comets, and meteors

Asteroids are large chunks of rock and are also called minor planets. They are found mainly between the orbits of Mars and Jupiter. Comets also orbit the sun, but travel in long, oval-shaped paths. Most of the time, comets are millions of miles beyond the outermost planet. Meteors are tiny pieces of dust or rock scattered through the solar system.

Gravity

The solar system is held together by the force of *gravity*. This is the force that makes an apple drop toward the earth when it falls from a tree. In the same way, the sun's gravitational force attracts the planets, asteroids, comets, and meteors toward itself, so that they do not fly off into space. Similarly, the gravitational force of a planet keeps its moons from flying away.

Earth year

The time taken for a planet to go around the sun is called a year. The length of the year is different for each planet. The closer a planet is to the sun, the faster it moves around it. Because it is so close to the sun, Mercury takes only 88 earth days to go around it. Jupiter, by contrast, takes nearly 12 earth years to go around the sun, and faraway Pluto takes 248 earth years.

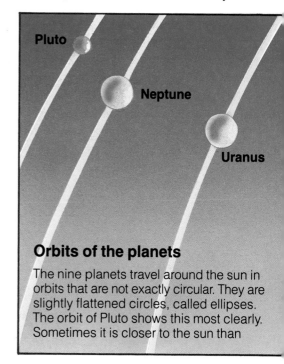

Orbits of the planets

The nine planets travel around the sun in orbits that are not exactly circular. They are slightly flattened circles, called ellipses. The orbit of Pluto shows this most clearly. Sometimes it is closer to the sun than

SCIENCE DISCOVERY

Revolution in astronomy

Born in Poland in 1473, Nicolaus Copernicus was the first person to show that the earth and other planets moved around the sun. He was a priest who developed an interest in astronomy. He studied the movements of the planets from the top of a tower, using simple instruments.

At this time, it was believed that the earth stood still and was the center of the universe. No one questioned this because the Church taught it. As a result, Copernicus did not publish his ideas for many years. Finally, he wrote a book which was printed just before he died in 1543. The book was banned by the Church because it was different from their beliefs, but Copernicus was eventually proved right.

Day and night

As a planet moves around the sun, it also rotates, or spins like a top, once a day. This causes day and night. Day length is different on each planet. An earth day is 23 hours 56 minutes long. On Mercury, it lasts 59 earth days and on Venus, 243 earth days.

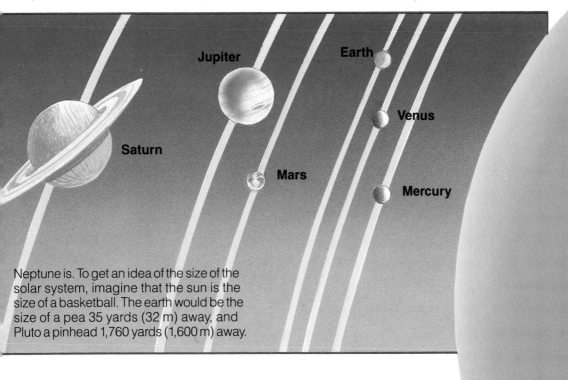

Neptune is. To get an idea of the size of the solar system, imagine that the sun is the size of a basketball. The earth would be the size of a pea 35 yards (32 m) away, and Pluto a pinhead 1,760 yards (1,600 m) away.

THE INNER PLANETS

The sun's family of planets splits into two groups. The first group contains the inner planets: Mercury, Venus, earth, and Mars. These planets are fairly small and rocky. The other group of planets are the outer planets: Jupiter, Saturn, Uranus, and Neptune. These giant planets are made mostly of gases. Pluto remains a mystery planet.

Mercury

Mercury is not much bigger than our moon. It is a lifeless and unchanging world, 36,250,000 miles (58 million km) from the sun. It has no air or water. The temperature is so high during the day that it could melt metal. But at night it is freezing. The surface is covered with craters formed by meteors hitting the planet. There are also mountains and plains formed by molten rock that came to the surface and hardened.

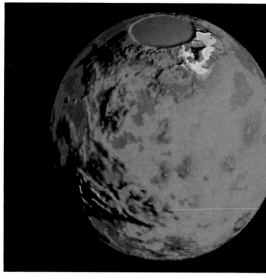

The bleak, stony landscape of Venus is veiled in clouds of sulfuric acid.

This shows an artist's idea of the surface of Mercury. The planet gets very hot during the day and very cold at night. The sky looks black because there is no atmosphere around Mercury.

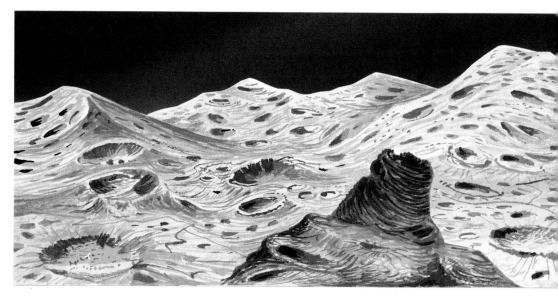

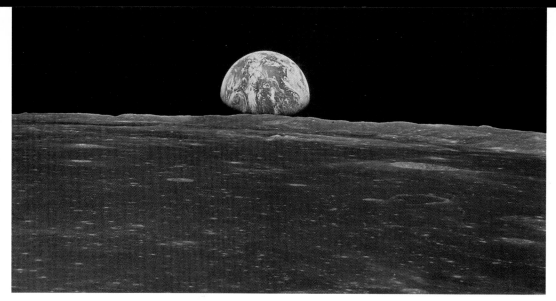

This picture of the earth rising over the horizon of the moon was photographed from the spacecraft Apollo 11.

Venus

Venus is called the Evening Star because it can often be seen at sunset. But it is a planet and does not burn like a star.

Venus is roughly the same size as the earth and is 67,500,000 miles (108 million km) from the sun. It has an atmosphere, but the main gas is carbon dioxide. The atmosphere traps heat and makes the planet even hotter than Mercury. There is no water. The brilliant clouds are made of acid, and lightning never stops flashing across the sky.

Earth

The earth is the third planet from the sun. It has the right temperature for life, plenty of water, and breathable air. It is 93,750,000 miles (150 million km) from the sun, and has a diameter of 8,000 miles (12,700 km).

Olympus Mons, the great volcano on Mars, is three times as high as Mount Everest on earth.

Mars

Mars, called the Red Planet, is 142,500,000 miles (228 million km) from the sun. Once people thought that there were deserts, seas, and canals on Mars. But photographs from spacecraft showed that Mars is rocky and cold with ice, but no liquid.

Mars has the largest known volcano in the solar system, Olympus Mons. It is about 15½ miles (25 km) high and 350 miles (550 km) across. Mars also has huge canyons. One is 2,500 miles (4,000 km) long and 45 miles (70 km) across. Mars has two tiny moons, called Phobos and Deimos.

THE OUTER PLANETS

Beyond Mars is the asteroid belt. Asteroids are large chunks of rock, probably left over from the time when the planets formed. There are thousands of asteroids. The largest, Ceres, is about 600 miles (1,000 km) across.

Jupiter

Jupiter is 490,000,000 miles (778 million km) from the sun, about five times the distance between the earth and the sun. It is the largest planet in the solar system, with a diameter of 88,750 miles (142,000 km). It weighs more than twice the other planets put together. Because it is so far from the sun, its surface is very cold. Yet inside, Jupiter is warm because the enormous pressure at the center of the giant planet generates heat.

The surface of Jupiter is made up of clouds of gas that form a number of dark belts and bright zones. There is one famous feature, called the Great Red Spot, that is believed to be an enormous storm. It covers an area 15,000 miles (25,000 km) long and 9,000 miles (14,000 km) wide. Jupiter has 16 moons, three of them larger than our moon. The one called Io is red and has large volcanoes.

Saturn

The next planet out from the sun is Saturn. It is a giant planet, almost as big as Jupiter, and it, too, is made of gas. There are belts of clouds as on Jupiter, but Saturn is a much cooler place, and its atmosphere is less stormy.

Saturn has a beautiful set of rings around it. These rings are made up

The planet Saturn has a beautiful system of rings, made of small pieces of orbiting ice. The rings are 175,000 miles (280,000 km) in diameter, which is three-quarters of the distance from the earth to the moon. One of Saturn's many moons is seen orbiting the planet.

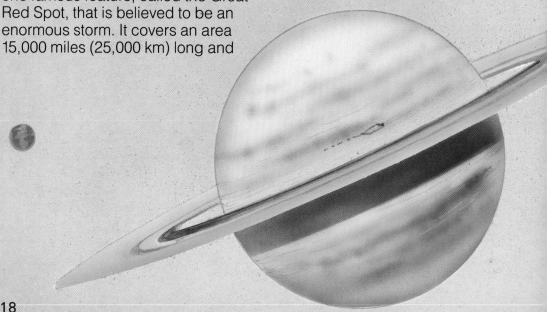

of particles of dust and ice circling the planet and are only a few miles thick. The largest of Saturn's many moons, called Titan, has an atmosphere, but it is so cold that no life can survive there.

Uranus

The next planet from the sun is Uranus. It is 1,800 million miles (2,870 million km) from the sun, and takes 84 earth years to complete each orbit. Uranus is about four times bigger than the earth. It is unusual because, unlike the other planets, it spins on its side instead of in an "upright" position. Therefore, as it orbits the sun, first one pole and then the other points toward the sun. This means that each pole has a day of 42 years, followed by an equally long night.

A close-up photograph of the giant planet Jupiter, taken from the spacecraft Voyager 1 in 1979, also shows two of the planet's moons, Io and Europa. The Great Red Spot is visible on the planet's surface.

Neptune

The last big planet is Neptune. This giant is 2,811 million miles (4,497 million km) from the sun, and is similar in size to Uranus. Its orbit takes 165 years.

Pluto

Far out in the solar system, about 40 times the distance from the earth to the sun, is Pluto. This planet is smaller than our moon and, because it is so far away, little is known about it. It may be rocky like Mars and Mercury, with a frosty coating. Some astronomers believe that it may be an "escaped" moon of Neptune.

COMETS AND METEORS

Comets are sometimes called "dirty snowballs." At their center is a ball of ice, rock, frozen gases, and dust. This ball, called the nucleus of the comet, moves around the sun. But a comet's path around the sun is not like a planet's orbit. Instead, its path forms a long, flattened loop. Most of the time, the comet travels in the farthest reaches of the solar system, but at regular intervals the comet's path brings it in closer to the sun. As it approaches the sun, it gets warmer, and some of the ice turns into gas. The gas and dust

Comet West was a spectacular comet that appeared in 1976. It sped past the earth, displaying a magnificent tail of gas and dust 30 million miles (50 million km) long.

form a tail which can stretch 60 million miles (100 million km) from the comet's head.

Halley's Comet

One of the most famous comets is Halley's comet. It was named for a famous English astronomer, Edmond Halley. He was the first to realize that comets orbit the sun. Halley's comet takes 76 years to go around the sun. It last appeared in 1986.

A comet is one of the most beautiful sights in the night sky. Comets do not flash, but move slowly across the sky from night to night. However, these sights are not very common. There have been few bright comets in the last fifty years.

The most famous comet

Born in 1656, Edmond Halley was thought of as the greatest astronomer of his time. He was a friend of the famous scientist Isaac Newton, and helped Newton to publish his results. Halley was made Astronomer Royal, the King's astronomer, in 1720 at the age of 64. He died in 1743.

He is best remembered for discovering that comets follow orbits around the sun. He predicted that a comet he saw in 1682 would return in 1758. When the comet did appear as predicted, it was named for him.

Halley also studied the earth's magnetic

field, tides, weather, and the way air pressure changes with height. He also invented diving equipment and formed a company to salvage shipwrecks.

Shooting stars

If you see a streak of light in the night sky, it will not be a comet, but a meteor, or "shooting star." Astronomers believe that meteors are particles of dust left behind by a comet. Most of them are smaller than pinheads. We would never see any of them unless they fell into the earth's atmosphere. When this happens, they burn quickly, which causes the streak of light which we call a shooting star – a misleading name, because they are not stars.

Meteorites

Occasionally, bigger pieces of rock enter the earth's atmosphere and hit the ground without burning up completely. They are called *meteorites* and are thought to be fragments of asteroids that have broken up. The largest meteorite known weighed over 60 tons and fell

in South Africa. In Arizona, there is a large crater made by a meteorite. It is 575 feet (175 m) deep and 4,175 feet (1,265 m) across.

This composite photograph of the Manicouagan Reservoir in Quebec, Canada, was taken by Landsat 1. It is believed to be a meteorite crater and is about 40 miles (65 km) wide.

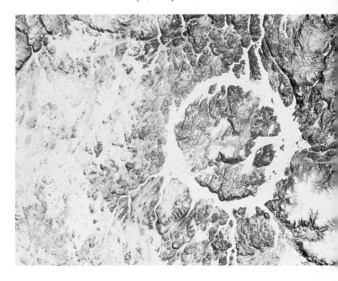

The moon and the planets

The moon is easy to study because it reflects sunlight. You do not need any equipment, although binoculars or a telescope will give you a better view, and a map of the moon's surface would be helpful.

STEP **1**

Study the moon every day for a month. Draw the shape, or phase, of the moon and note down the date. For part of the month, the moon cannot be seen. This is because it is between the sun and the earth, and so its unlit side is facing the earth. This is called a New Moon. As the moon orbits the earth, the lit-up face gradually becomes visible. For the first few days, it appears as a thin crescent. After 7 days, half the moon's face is lit up. This is called the first quarter. At Full Moon, the moon is on the opposite side of the earth from the sun and its entire surface is lit up. Work out how many days after the New Moon the Full Moon occurs. When will the next New Moon occur?

1 2 3 4 5 6 7 8

1 New Moon **2** Crescent Moon **3** First quarter
4 Gibbous Moon **5** Full Moon **6** Gibbous Moon
7 Last Quarter **8** Crescent Moon

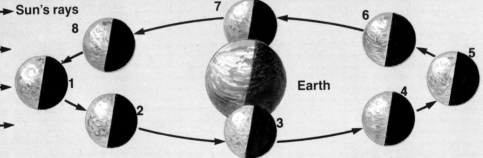

Sun's rays

Earth

Moon's orbit around the earth

Sea of Rains

Sea of Tranquillity

Ocean of Storms

Sea of Vapors

Sea of Moisture

STEP **2**

Get to know the names of some of the plains, mountains, and craters on the moon. They are best seen when they are near the boundary between light and dark. At this time they throw longer shadows and are easier to see. Don't forget to make sketches of everything you see.

STEP 3

The planets are the wanderers of the night sky, so it is not always easy to find them. Sometimes, there are maps of the stars in newspapers showing the positions of the planets each month. There are five planets that can be seen with the naked eye – Mercury, Venus, Mars, Jupiter, and Saturn.

Mercury is never easy to see with the naked eye. Look for it in the western sky after sunset, or in the eastern sky before dawn.

Venus is always bright, because its clouds reflect sunlight very well. Look for it in the west after sunset or in the east before dawn. It looks like a bright star and can sometimes be seen before sunset. With a small telescope, you will see that Venus has phases like the moon.

Mars looks red compared to other objects in the sky. The best time to see Mars is when it is opposite the sun in the sky and is then closest to earth.

Mercury

Venus

Earth

Mars

Jupiter

Saturn

Jupiter is far away, but it is so large that you can just see it without binoculars. With binoculars, you will be able to see a disk of light. A small telescope will show you a yellowish, flattened disk crossed by dark lines. You will also be able to see the four largest moons. Watch how they change position from night to night as they orbit the planet.

You can just see **Saturn** without binoculars. To see the rings of Saturn, you will need a telescope with a lens at least 25 inches (60 mm) across. When the rings are flat, they are very hard to see, but when they are tilted toward us, Saturn is a splendid sight.

Observing the sun

The sun is an interesting, but dangerous object to study. **Never** look directly at the sun even through a telescope or binoculars with a dark filter over the eyepiece; **you may permanently damage your eyes**. Always project the sun's image either onto a sheet of paper held behind the eyepiece, or into a black box mounted on the eyepiece. Point the telescope toward the sun; **do not** look through the eyepiece while you remove the lens cap. Move the telescope until the sun's image appears on the paper. Look for sunspots and partial eclipses.

WHAT KIND OF STAR?

The sun is the nearest star to earth and the only one that astronomers can study in detail. They have learned that the sun, like most stars, is a huge ball of very hot gas. Vast amounts of energy are produced by nuclear reactions deep within its center. This description fits most, if not all, stars, but there are different kinds of stars to be observed.

Some stars have companions. Sometimes pairs of stars, called **double stars** or **binaries**, circle around each other. Sometimes there are three or more stars moving around each other.

Stars are also found in larger groups, called clusters. Some clusters form great ball-shaped clouds of stars. Others have no definite shape. The largest groups are called galaxies. Our own galaxy – the **Milky Way** – is a typical galaxy. It contains about 100,000 million stars, including the sun.

Compared to many stars, the sun is small. It is about 875,000 miles (1,400,000 km) across, a dwarf star. Betelgeuse, in the constellation of Orion, is a supergiant. It is 300 times bigger. Stars vary in brightness, size, and temperature. They also vary according to the stage in their "life" or development, they have reached.

Thousands of millions of years from now, our sun will become a red giant. This happens when a star has used up most of its nuclear energy. It swells up and cools. Eventually, it will throw off its outer layer and become a very small star called a **white dwarf**.

Some large stars explode when they run out of "fuel." These exploding stars are called **supernovae**. They are very rare, so astronomers were very excited

when, in 1987, a bright supernova occurred, enabling them to study it. There is another type of exploding star, called a *nova*. A nova is quite different from a supernova. A nova is a faint star that suddenly becomes brighter and then, after a few weeks or months, fades away again.

THE LIFE OF A STAR

A star is born inside a cloud of gas and dust called a nebula. The force of gravity attracts together some of the dust particles, and a small, ball-shaped object is formed. At first, it is cold, but gravity continues to squeeze the dust particles together, and the ball heats up. Eventually, it is so hot that nuclear reactions, which convert matter into energy, occur. The star begins to shine.

Nuclear fuel

Nuclear reactions use up the material from which the star was formed and produce light and heat. So the star gets lighter all the time. Most stars have enough nuclear "fuel" to last for thousands of millions of years.

What happens when a star runs out of fuel depends on how large it is. A dwarf star like our sun starts to swell.

The star expands to become a red giant. Eventually, the cool outer layers of the star are thrown off. The center part of the star becomes a small, heavy white dwarf. It shines weakly for a very long time. Then it cools down and fades, until it stops shining completely and becomes a dead star, a black dwarf.

Supernova

Larger stars use up their nuclear fuel sooner than smaller stars. Then they cool down and expand to become red supergiants. Next comes a giant explosion, a supernova, which throws most of the star's material off into space. It produces an enormous flash of light and energy. From earth, the star would appear to become very bright.

There are two possible outcomes of such an explosion: a *neutron star* or a

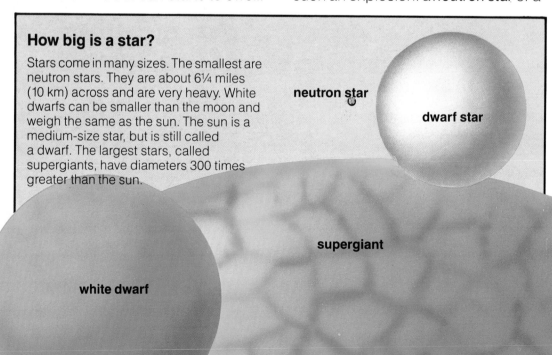

How big is a star?

Stars come in many sizes. The smallest are neutron stars. They are about 6¼ miles (10 km) across and are very heavy. White dwarfs can be smaller than the moon and weigh the same as the sun. The sun is a medium-size star, but is still called a dwarf. The largest stars, called supergiants, have diameters 300 times greater than the sun.

neutron star

dwarf star

supergiant

white dwarf

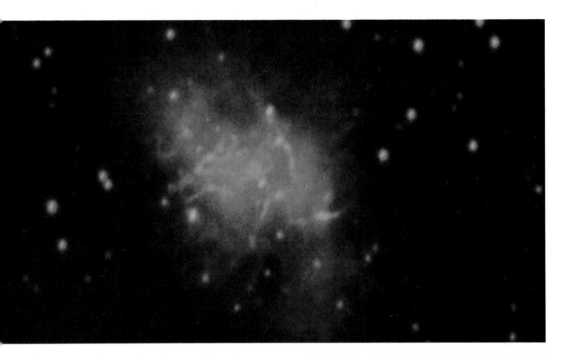

The Crab nebula contains the remains of a supernova explosion that took place in 1054. It was so bright that it could be seen during daylight. In the center of the cloud is a neutron star that sends out pulses of radio waves as it spins more than thirty times a second.

black hole. A neutron star is like an egg – small with a hard shell. Inside, there is a very heavy kind of liquid. They often spin very quickly, and as they spin, they send out pulses of radio energy. For this reason, they are called *pulsars*.

Black holes

A black hole is a point in space where gravity is so strong that not even light can escape. It is made of very dense material. A black hole less than ½ inch (1 cm) across would weigh the same as the earth. It is believed that the supernova seen in 1987 produced a neutron star.

Star colors

Stars vary in size, and therefore in temperature and brightness. The color of a star shows how hot it is. White stars like Sirius are hotter than yellow stars like our sun. Red stars like Betelgeuse are cooler than yellow stars.

The light from a star also gives us some idea about which gases are in the star. A physicist can split up the light received from a star, like a rainbow. This is called the spectrum of the star. There are lots of dark lines across a star's spectrum and the position of these lines, rather like a fingerprint, identifies which gases are present. This is the sun's spectrum.

STAR GROUPS

Stars in our galaxy are often found in groups, or clusters. Sometimes the groups contain many stars. Globular clusters are groups of stars that form a tight ball shape. There may be millions of stars in a globular cluster. In the center, the stars are so close together that they cannot be seen separately, even with a big telescope. The best globular clusters visible to the naked eye are in the southern sky and cannot be seen from northern Europe or most of North America. But in the constellation of Hercules, there is one, known as M13, that shows up well through binoculars.

This globular ball-shaped cluster of stars (at the bottom of the photo) is in the constellation of Centaurus. Halley's comet can be seen at the top.

Other clusters are loosely shaped and are called open clusters. They contain a few dozen stars, as in the Pleiades (a cluster in the constellation Taurus), or many thousands of stars.

Star pairs

Often, stars are found in pairs. The stars in the pair revolve around each other in the same way as the ends of a dumbbell revolve around each other when the bell is turned. These pairs are called double, or binary, stars.

For example, Mizar, in the Big Dipper, is one of a pair. It has a companion star, called Alcor, which you can see on a clear night. Mizar and Alcor take millions of years to move around each other even though they appear close together. With a telescope you can also see that Mizar itself is not a single star, but two stars very close together.

Variable brightness

Sometimes stars seem to vary in brightness. One reason may be that a bright star and a faint star are circling each other. When the faint star passes in front, the light reaching us is reduced, and the star seems to dim.

Cepheid variables vary in brightness. They are pulsating stars that expand and contract at regular intervals. When they expand, they become less bright. Other variable stars are unpredictable. Some, like flare stars, increase their brightness over a matter of minutes because of outbursts on the star's surface. Other variable stars become

SCIENCE DISCOVERY

Measuring distances

Distances in astronomy are measured by parallax, the apparent shift in the position of an object as seen from two different places. You can try this for yourself. Hold your thumb up, level with your eyes. Look at your thumb against the scene in front of you, first with your right eye and then with your left. Your thumb will appear to shift against the background.

Parallax measurements can be used to calculate distance because the amount of shift in position depends on the distance of the object from the observer.

The distance of a star from earth can be calculated in the same way. Sightings of a planet against the background stars are taken six months apart when the earth is on

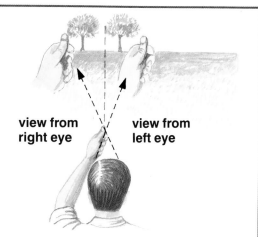

view from right eye **view from left eye**

opposite sides of its orbit. The apparent shift in the star's position in relation to the background stars is used to calculate its distance. The unit of measurement is called the parsec (parallax second) and one parsec is equal to 19½ million million miles (31 million million km), or 3·26 light years.

brighter over a period of months. Within days, a nova or supernova may show an enormous increase in brightness as the star explodes.

When a faint star revolves around a brighter one, the dull star blocks out some of the light as it passes in front of the bright star. The brightness of the pair is greatest when light is reaching earth from both stars at the same time.

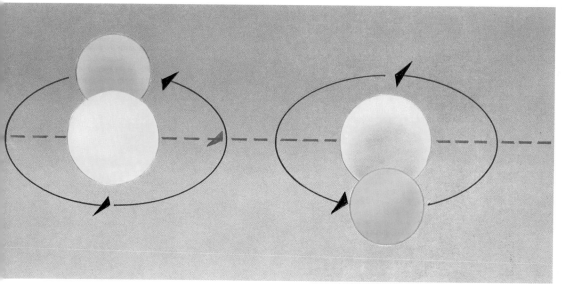

NEBULAE AND GALAXIES

On a clear night, you can see small, faint, misty patches of light in the sky. A telescope would reveal these to be clouds of gas and dust called nebulae. The word "nebula" is Latin for cloud. A well-known nebula that you can see with the naked eye is in the "sword" of Orion, the Hunter, below the three stars of his belt.

Star birth

Some nebulae glow because, inside them, stars are being born. The light given out by these stars makes the surrounding dust cloud glow. We see other nebulae because they reflect light from nearby stars. However, some nebulae are dark and do not glow. In fact, they are so dark that they block out the light from stars behind them. A sharp-eyed observer might also see, on a clear night, faint patches of light called galaxies. A galaxy is a huge group of stars that is so far away that its light takes millions of years to reach us. Even the largest telescopes cannot see the separate stars in very distant galaxies. A typical galaxy contains 100,000 million stars. Often the stars are arranged in a beautiful spiral pattern, like a pinwheel.

The Milky Way

We call our galaxy the Milky Way. Our solar system lies two-thirds of the way to the edge of the galaxy, in one of the spiral arms. When we look toward the galaxy, or along the spiral arms, we see many, many stars. This huge number of closely-packed stars is visible as a band of misty light across the night sky.

The Horsehead nebula is an odd-shaped nebula made of dark dust that blocks out light from the brighter nebula behind it.

SCIENCE DISCOVERY

An amazing discovery has been made about galaxies. Except for a few of the nearest ones, all galaxies are moving away from us. This means that the Universe is getting bigger all the time. Just why this is happening is a puzzle, but one thing is clear. In the past, the galaxies must have been closer together. Scientists have worked out that about 15 thousand million years ago, all the galaxies must have been very close together. Most scientists think that there was an enormous explosion, which created the universe and caused the galaxies to move apart. This original explosion is known as the "*Big Bang.*"

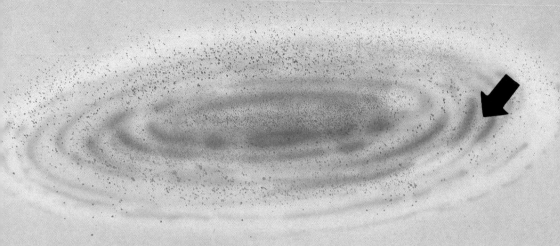

Light years away

The nearest spiral galaxy to ours is called the Andromeda galaxy. It is about 12½ million million million miles (20 million million million km) away. The distances to other galaxies is so huge that astronomers measure large distances in *"light years"*: the distance that a beam of light travels in one year.

Our galaxy, the Milky Way, consists of a vast spiral containing 100,000 million stars. The position of the solar system is shown by the arrow.

Light travels at about 187,500 miles (300,000 km) every second, 5½ million million miles (9 million million km) a year. The Andromeda galaxy is about 2 million light years away.

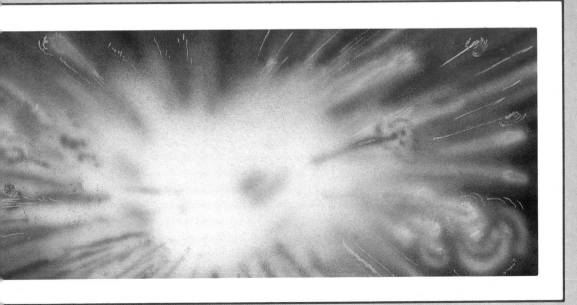

Although a telescope is necessary to get a really good view, some galaxies and nebulae can be seen with the naked eye. You can also learn to recognize beautiful star clusters.

STEP 2

One of the stars in Perseus is called Algol. This is a variable star. Every three days, Algol fades and brightens within a few hours. This is because a dull companion star is orbiting Algol and blocks out the light as it passes between the earth and Algol. You might be able to see this change if you note how bright Algol is, compared with nearby stars. Do this each time you are star-gazing, and you might spot Algol as it fades.

PROJECT 5

A Royal Family

Start by exploring the stars around the constellations of Cassiopeia, Cepheus, and Andromeda. All three can be found together in the northern sky.

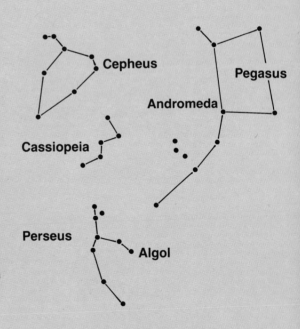

Cepheus

Pegasus

Andromeda

Cassiopeia

Perseus

Algol

STEP 1

Find Cassiopeia by following an imaginary line from the Big Dipper to the North Star. Cepheus lies almost between Cassiopeia and the North Star. Andromeda is farther away from the North Star than Cassiopeia. The Great Square of Pegasus is on one side of Andromeda. Perseus is on the other.

STEP 3

In the constellation of Andromeda is the great spiral galaxy of Andromeda, just visible with the naked eye. It looks like a small, fuzzy patch of light. This is the most distant object visible to the unaided eye. It is more than 2·2 million light years away.

6

The Hunter and the Bull

Now explore the sky around the constellation of Orion, the Hunter. To find Orion itself, look back at Project 2 on page 9. Remember, it can only be seen during the winter months.

STEP 1

Find Orion. Just below the three stars that form the belt, you will see the sword of Orion. At the bottom of the sword is a small star. Just above this star, you will see a faint patch of light. This can easily be seen with the naked eye. With binoculars, you will see that it is a nebula of shining gas. It is the Great Nebula of Orion, which is probably the best known of all the nebulae. It is about 1,000 light years away. Inside the cloud of gas, stars are being born.

STEP 2

Now find the constellation of Taurus, the Bull. If you look north, following an imaginary line from Orion's belt, you will come to a bright, faintly red star called Aldebaran. This is the brightest star in Taurus.

STEP 3

Two beautiful groups of stars are to be found near Aldebaran. These are the Pleiades and the Hyades. The Pleiades form a tiny pan-like shape. You should be able to see six of the seven main stars with the naked eye. The Hyades make a small triangle shape close to Aldebaran. Both are open clusters.

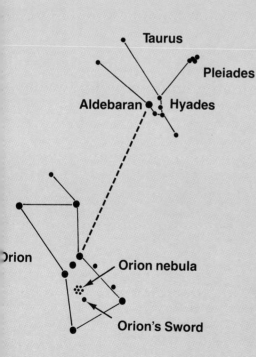

According to an ancient story, the Pleiades were the seven daughters of Atlas, who were turned into stars. The seventh sister is invisible. She is said to be hiding in shame because she loved a man and not a god. The Hyades were half-sisters of the Pleiades. They wept because of their brother Hyas' death. This story may have been based on the fact that the rainy season starts in parts of Europe when the Hyades appear.

ASTRONOMY TODAY

T he modern astronomer uses a great deal of highly technical equipment. The best telescopes used today are computer-controlled and use highly sensitive cameras and electronic equipment to record what they see. The modern astronomer does not spend time looking through a telescope. Indeed, the telescope may not even be in the same country as the astronomer. Communications satellites can be used by an astronomer in one country to monitor the stars through a telescope on a mountaintop in the other hemisphere.

In addition to telescopes that gather light, the modern astronomer uses telescopes that collect radio waves. These are called *radio telescopes*, and they have been used to make many important discoveries. For instance, they were used to identify the most far-away objects ever detected, called *quasars*. Several radio telescopes can be linked together to produce very detailed radio "pictures" of objects in far distant parts of the universe.

Satellites high above the earth are used in modern astronomy, too. Sometimes they carry telescopes that detect heat or X-rays. There are plans to put a large telescope, called the Hubble Space Telescope, into orbit around the earth. When this happens, astronomers will have an important new tool.

Spacecraft can carry cameras and other equipment to study the planets they pass by. Space probes have been sent to all the planets except Pluto.

They have sent back many beautiful pictures of our neighbors in space. A probe was also sent to study Halley's comet when it last returned in 1986.

This is a line of radio telescopes in the desert near Socorro, New Mexico. These telescopes receive radio waves instead of light. By combining the signals received by many telescopes, astronomers can "see" very faint objects and study distant parts of the universe.

Special telescopes are built deep underground. They look for tiny particles, *neutrinos*, that are produced by the sun and other stars. Neutrinos can travel through rock and penetrate deep into the earth. One such telescope detected neutrinos emitted from the supernova that exploded in 1987.

TELESCOPES AND OBSERVATORIES

The simplest kind of telescope has two pieces of clear glass called lenses, one at each end of a light-proof tube. The lenses have curved sides like a magnifying glass. The larger lens, the objective, is farthest from your eye. Light from the object you are viewing passes through the objective and down the tube. The smaller lens, the eyepiece, magnifies the image to give you a close-up view.

Upside down

This kind of telescope produces an upside-down image. Because of this, many telescopes have an extra lens in between the objective and the eyepiece to turn the image the right way up. Good-quality binoculars use triangular pieces of glass, called prisms, between the lenses. Telescopes which use a combination of lenses are known as refracting telescopes, or refractors for short.

Brighter images

Reflector telescopes use a curved mirror instead of an objective lens. Light passes down the telescope tube to the mirror at the other end. The image of the object is then reflected by a smaller mirror into the eyepiece in the side of the tube. Most astronomers use reflecting telescopes because they are cheaper than refractors and can be made in larger sizes.

The bigger the mirror or objective lens in a telescope, the more light it collects. This makes a brighter image. Astronomers have made telescopes with bigger and bigger mirrors so that they can see faint light sources.

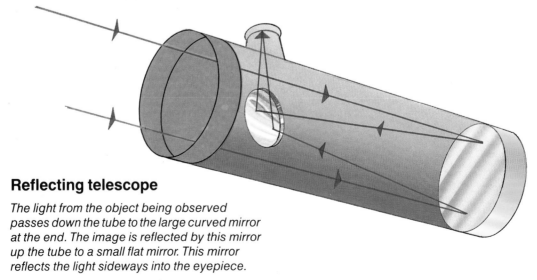

Reflecting telescope

The light from the object being observed passes down the tube to the large curved mirror at the end. The image is reflected by this mirror up the tube to a small flat mirror. This mirror reflects the light sideways into the eyepiece.

7

How to make a simple refracting telescope

You will need two cardboard tubes (one fitting inside the other), a large cork which will just fit into the narrower of the two cardboard tubes, some modeling clay and a sharp knife. You will also need two lenses, one small one, with a focal length of ¾ to

1¼ inches (2 to 3 cm), which fits in the cork and a larger lens, with a focal length of 10 to 12 inches (25 to 30 cm), which will fit in the wider cardboard tube. Lenses from an old pair of binoculars or magnifying glasses might be suitable, or buy them from an optician or from a specialist hobby store.

STEP 2

Place the large lens with the longer focal length in the end of the wider cardboard tube. Fix it firmly in place with the clay. Make sure that the lens is upright.

STEP 3

Slide the narrow cardboard tube into the wider tube. Look through the eyepiece at an object some distance away. Slide the narrow tube in or out until the object is in focus and can be seen clearly. If you find it difficult to focus your telescope, make sure that both lenses are upright and in line with one another. With a little practice, you should soon be able to use your telescope to help you look at the stars and planets.

STEP 1

First, make the eyepiece of the telescope. Cut a hole in the cork just large enough for the small lens to fit into. Ask an adult to help you. Secure the small lens in place with modeling clay. Make sure that it is upright. Push the cork into one end of the narrow cardboard tube.

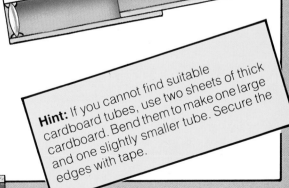

Hint: If you cannot find suitable cardboard tubes, use two sheets of thick cardboard. Bend them to make one large and one slightly smaller tube. Secure the edges with tape.

EXPLORING THE PLANETS

Astronomers have made many discoveries about our planetary neighbors in space by using space probes. These are spacecraft that are launched from earth using rockets. They take cameras and other instruments into space and radio back information about what they find.

the U.S.S.R. launched Luna 1. It missed the moon by 3,750 miles (6,000 km), but the next attempt, Luna 2, was successful eight months later. It hit the moon and became the first man-made object to "visit" another world. Since then, space probes have visited all the planets except Pluto.

Crash after launch

Pioneer 1, launched by the United States in 1958, started it all. Pioneer 1 failed to reach the moon as intended. It crashed into the Pacific Ocean two days after it was launched. Failures were common in the early days of space exploration. In January, 1959,

Exploring Venus

In 1975, the Soviet Union sent two probes, Venera 9 and Venera 10, to explore Venus, the nearest planet to

This is how an artist imagined the Pioneer 11 probe approaching Saturn in 1979 after a six-year journey to the planet. Pioneer 11 also visited Jupiter on the way.

earth. Both spacecraft landed on the surface of Venus and sent back good television pictures.

In 1975, the U.S. sent Viking 1 and Viking 2 to Mars. After they had landed, a mechanical arm on the probes scooped up samples of rock and soil. They tested the soil, but discovered no traces of life. The probes sent back the first pictures from the surface of Mars.

Jupiter visit

In 1977, the U.S. launched two probes called Voyager 1 and Voyager 2. They reached Jupiter in 1979 and sent back many pictures of Jupiter and its moons. Then they headed for Saturn and photographed it. Voyager 1 then turned up and away from the solar system. Voyager 2 flew on to the next planet, Uranus, which it reached and photographed in 1986. Then it went on to Neptune. Voyager will not be able to reach Pluto, which will remain unexplored for the time being.

Comet fly-by

Space probes can also be used to explore comets. When Halley's comet returned in 1986, a probe called Giotto flew close by it. Giotto sent back many pictures and valuable information about the comet. There are plans to put a large telescope, the Hubble Space Telescope, into orbit. Astronomers will then be able to see much farther into space. Manned space stations will also provide valuable observatories.

The Voyager spacecraft

This probe was equipped for numerous scientific tasks. Cameras took detailed pictures. Other instruments measured the magnetic fields of Jupiter and Saturn and radiation in space surrounding the planets. Radio emissions from the planets were measured using the antenna. Information gathered was radioed back to earth, using the 11½ foot (3½-m) radio dish.

BECOME AN ASTRONOMER

A planisphere shows the position of the stars at any time of year.

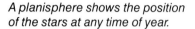

The best way to start is by joining an astronomy club. In a club, you will meet people who know their way around the sky. They will teach you a great deal. You might be able to use their equipment, such as telescopes. This will help you if you decide to buy your own equipment later. Some astronomy clubs have their own small observatory, where they hold regular observing sessions. Clubs often arrange talks by specialists and trips to observatories and other places of astronomical interest.

You should read all you can about astronomy. There are many books and magazines about the stars. Some books contain maps of the stars, showing exactly which stars and planets can be seen at any time.

Either a small refracting telescope, like the one shown, or a reflector are suitable for the amateur astronomer.

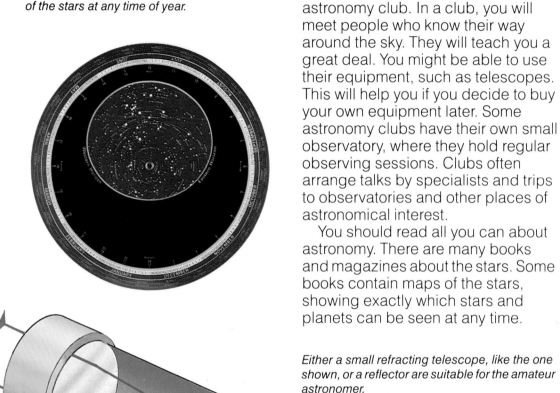

lens

lens

light rays

eyepiece

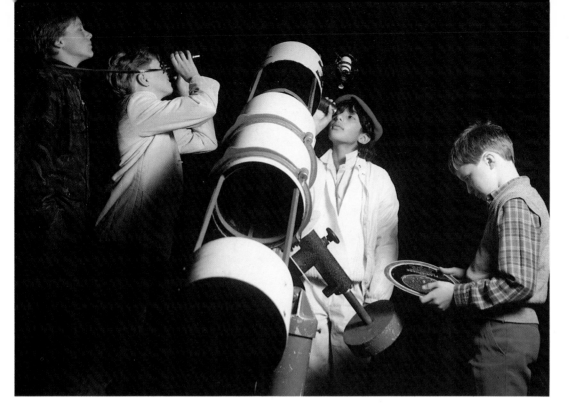

You could also buy or borrow a planisphere. This is made of two circular pieces of plastic. The bottom piece has a map of the heavens printed on it. The top piece of plastic has the days of the year printed on it. You turn the top piece to the date you want, and it will show you which stars you can expect to see on that date.

If possible, visit a planetarium. This is like a movie theater with the screen on the roof. A projector shines small points of light onto the screen to represent the stars. The points of light are moved around to show how the stars move. Some planetariums take you on an imaginary trip through space to visit faraway star systems.

Binoculars are the best equipment for the amateur astronomer to start with. You should choose binoculars marked 7 x 50. This means the image viewed through a 50 mm lens will be magnified

These children are using a 8½ inch (21-cm) reflecting telescope for close-up views of the planets, nebulae, and galaxies. One is using binoculars, which give good wide-angle views of bright nebulae and stars. They are using a planisphere to show which stars are visible.

7 times. They will not be too heavy to hold steady, although a tripod or clamp to hold them is also useful. Binoculars open up the sky, enabling you to see many more stars, like double stars and nebulae. Craters on the moon, and even the moons of Jupiter, become visible.

Choosing your first telescope can be difficult because of the cost. Refractors, which use lenses, are more expensive than reflectors, which use mirrors. For this reason, most beginners choose a reflecting telescope. Choose carefully, and get advice from other amateurs before you decide.

WHY DOES...?

Why does a star twinkle?

Have you ever noticed the shimmering heat rising from the ground on a hot day? This shimmering effect is caused by the swirling of the heated air as it rises off the hot ground. Rays of light passing through this swirling heat become twisted and distorted, and objects look as if they're wobbling. The same thing happens to rays of light coming through space and through the earth's atmosphere. The source of light in the star is steady, but by the time we see it, it has been distorted so the star seems to "twinkle."

What is an eclipse?

Sometimes on its path around the earth, the moon passes between the earth and the sun. Although the moon is much smaller than the sun, it is relatively close to the earth and is able to block out much of the sun's light. When the sun is completely blotted out, it is called a total *eclipse*. If the sun is only partly covered, it is called a partial eclipse. A third kind of eclipse occurs when the moon is slightly farther from the earth and therefore appears smaller. This is called an annular eclipse. When this happens, all but the outer edge of the sun is obscured, and the moon has a ring of light around it.

The moon is visible because it reflects light from the sun. When the earth

Solar eclipse

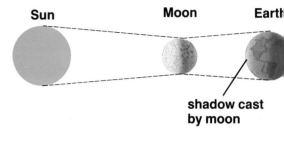

Sun   Moon   Earth

shadow cast by moon

Lunar eclipse

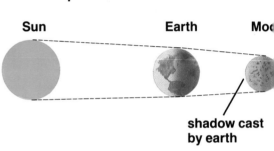

Sun   Earth   Moon

shadow cast by earth

moves between the sun and the moon, the moon is in shadow and goes dark. This is called an eclipse of the moon.

How many stars are there?

If you look at the sky on a clear night away from bright city lights, you can see about 2,500 stars. A small telescope or a pair of binoculars will reveal many more. The large telescopes used by professional astronomers show that there are countless numbers of stars in the universe. However, astronomers have made estimates, or guesses, of the number of stars. It is estimated that there are about 1,000 million galaxies in the universe. Each galaxy contains about 100,000 million stars. So, if these estimates are correct, there are 100 million million million stars in the universe!

Is there life in space?

We can be sure that there is no other life in our solar system. The moon has no air; Venus is unsuitable in every way; the giant planets have no firm surface and are made mostly of hydrogen. Mars is the most suitable planet for life, but space probes have landed on Mars and found no evidence of life.

Some people think that there must be life somewhere in space. There are so many stars, they argue, that there must be some stars with planets circling around them, and some of those planets must have water and air and living creatures. If there are living creatures on other planets, we cannot communicate with them yet. The distances in the universe are too great for us to talk to distant planets.

Scientists are always listening and watching for signs of life in other parts of the universe. Space probes that have left our solar system carry details of life here on earth, but if there is anybody out there, we are unlikely to make contact in our lifetime.

How far away are the stars?

The closest star to us is the sun. It is 93,750,000 miles (150 million km) from the earth. The next closest star is in the constellation of Centaurus. It is called Proxima Centauri and is 4 light years away. This is a long way. If the distance between the sun and the earth was 3¼ inches (5 cm), Proxima Centauri would be 7½ miles (12 km) away.

The most distant objects detected from earth are called *quasars*. They are objects that are smaller than galaxies, but give out tremendous amounts of radio energy. Some scientists think that quasars may be giant black holes. Because of their great energy output, quasars can be "seen" with radio telescopes even though they are so far away. The most distant quasar is thought to be about 13,000 million light years away.

The Orion Nebula is about 1,600 light years from earth. It is fan-shaped and spreads across about 15 light years.

THINGS TO REMEMBER

What the words mean....

Here are explanations of some of the words in this book that you may find unfamiliar. In some cases, they aren't the exact scientific definitions, because many of these are very complicated, but the descriptions should help you to understand some of the words that astronomers use.

ASTEROID A large chunk of rock orbiting the sun between the orbits of Mars and Jupiter.

BIG BANG The enormous explosion that scientists believe took place when the universe came into being.

BINARY STAR A double star system, made up of two stars, one of which is moving around the other, or both of which are orbiting a common center of gravity.

BLACK HOLE A very dense object whose force of gravity is so strong that not even rays of light can escape from it.

COMET A small body made of dust and gas that travels around the sun in an oval-shaped path.

CONSTELLATION A group of stars that form a pattern or shape in the sky as viewed from earth.

DOUBLE STAR see Binary Star.

ECLIPSE When one body in space throws its shadow onto another body in space.

GALAXY A huge group of stars in space.

GRAVITY The force of attraction that draws one body toward another.

LIGHT YEAR The distance light travels in one year, about 6 million million miles (9.5 million million km).

METEOR A fragment of rock or dust traveling around the sun that burns up on contact with the earth's atmosphere. Also called a "shooting star."

44

METEORITE A large meteor that does not completely burn up as it travels through the earth's atmosphere, and so hits the earth's surface.

MILKY WAY The name given to our galaxy and visible as the faint band of light crossing the night sky.

NEBULA A cloud of dust and gas in space.

NEUTRINO A tiny sub-atomic particle emitted by stars that can travel easily through solid material.

NEUTRON STAR A star made up of very heavy particles called neutrons.

NOVA A star that suddenly shines more brightly for a time.

NUCLEAR REACTION A process that changes the nature of particles of matter, releasing large amounts of energy as it does.

OBSERVATORY A building that houses telescopes and other astronomical instruments.

ORBIT The path of a planet, satellite, or other object as it moves around another body in space.

PLANET A cold body that orbits a star.

PROMINENCE A huge flame that bursts from the surface of the sun.

PULSAR A star that sends out regular bursts of radio waves or light.

QUASAR A very distant, star-like object that sends out very powerful radio waves.

RADIO TELESCOPE A telescope that collects radio waves instead of light.

SHOOTING STAR see Meteor.

SOLAR SYSTEM Our sun, and the planets, asteroids, comets, and other material that move around it.

SUNSPOT A dark patch on the surface of the sun.

SUPERGIANT The largest type of star.

SUPERNOVA The enormous explosion that occurs when a large star runs out of energy.

TELESCOPE An instrument used to observe distant objects more clearly.

UNIVERSE Everything that exists.

WHITE DWARF A small, heavy star.

INDEX